Power Food On the Go

PREPARE
PRESERVE &
TAKE ALONG

Rens Kroes

FAIR WINDS

Brimming with creative inspiration, how-to projects, and useful information to enrich your everyday life, Quarto Knows is a favorite destination for those pursuing their interests and passions. Visit our site and dig deeper with our books into your area of interest: Quarto Creates, Quarto Cooks, Quarto Homes, Quarto Lives, Quarto Drives, Quarto Explores, Quarto Gifts, or Quarto Kids.

First Published in the United States of America in 2017 by Fair Winds Press, an imprint of The Quarto Group, 100 Cummings Center, Suite 265-D, Beverly, MA 01915, USA.
T (978) 282-9590 F (978) 283-2742 QuartoKnows.com

Fair Winds Press titles are also available at discount for retail, wholesale, promotional, and bulk purchase. For details, contact the Special Sales Manager by email at specialsales@quarto.com or by mail at The Quarto Group, Attn: Special Sales Manager, 401 Second Avenue North, Suite 310, Minneapolis, MN 55401, USA.

21 20 19 18 17   1 2 3 4 5

ISBN: 978-1-59233- 782-8

Library of Congress Cataloging-in-Publication Data available

English Translation Jessica Kroezen
Design and Layout Bülent Yüksel, *www.bybulent.com*
Lifestyle Photography Anne Timmer
Styling Renske van der Ploeg
Makeup Cécile Holle
Post-production Neda Gueorguieva
Photography for Recipes and Spreads Lieke Heijn & Pim Janswaard, *www.cameronstudio.nl*
Culinary Creation Yvonne Jimmink & Jacqueline Pietrowski

Printed in China

With thanks to Lizet Sleutelberg, Tanja Terstappen, Yvonne Jimmink, Sandra de Cocq Productions, Kimberley Jade Bleeker, Rens Ganni, Iro, Just Franky, Modström, Nike, Pommantere, Salon Heleen Hulsman, the Darling, Toms, Zoe Karssen

Contents

We are all always on the go. Work hard, play hard has really become the norm for a lot of people. It means working hard, keeping up with an array of social obligations, and making sure to relax while you're at it. We run around like crazy. Oh yeah, and we also want to make sure that we are (and stay) fit and healthy. Our busy lives can be inspiring and can really amp up our energy, but when you're busy and on the go a lot, it can make it difficult to take good care of yourself. When you're on the go, you don't always have a kitchen at your disposal, which makes it even more difficult to maintain healthy eating habits. It's also very tempting to grab a quick snack somewhere en route.

What can I bring with me besides just a cheese sandwich in a plastic baggy? How do I resist unhealthy snacks when I'm out and about? How do I bring a salad to work? It's precisely these kinds of questions that inspired this book. It felt like the right moment to put my ideas and tips in writing.

I started experimenting with on-the-go recipes when I was quite young. I preferred to devote my allowance to things other than sausage rolls, energy drinks, and cookies. Since then, I have become quite creative in thinking up recipes and I've become pretty good at planning, prepping, and storing.

In this book, I share 62 delicious recipes that can all be taken on the go—whether it's to work, to the park, or to dinner with friends. Each recipe includes information on when the best time to prepare it is and how long it keeps. Of course, this all takes a bit of extra time and patience and a willingness to experiment, but spending part of an otherwise lazy Sunday in the kitchen, preparing your breakfast and lunch for the next day, makes it all very manageable. What's more, you'll be spending your time and energy on something that's good for you (and for your state of mind) and you'll feel it. You will create peace, become more creative in the kitchen, and be less inclined to succumb to the temptation to eat unhealthy food when you're out of the house.

That's reason enough to get started, right?

Happy prepping! Rens

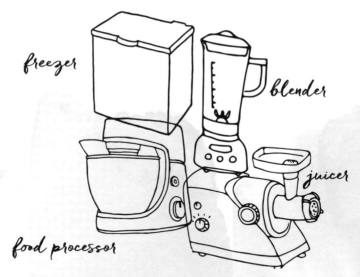

freezer

blender

juicer

food processor

Power Kitchen 1

*You don't need a fancy kitchen to cook **healthy** and take care of yourself—just **plan ahead**. These **tools** will help make your pursuit of **fresh** and healthy food a little **easier**—even in your tiny Amsterdam or New York kitchen. With the **right equipment**, you can turn any **kitchen** into a Power Kitchen.*

oven & stove

scale

spiralizer

Blender

A blender is probably the most important tool in the Power Kitchen, no matter how small it may be. You'll use it for your morning smoothie as well as for sauces, soups, and making the batter/dough for all sorts of sweets and snacks. For these Power Food recipes, I use an 800-watt blender.

Oven & Stove

You really do need an oven. Particularly if you want to make large quantities of certain things to store. The type of oven or stove is up to you. Whatever works. I prefer to cook on gas and use a convection oven, but there are many people who do just fine with an electric stove and a mini counter-top toaster oven.

Freezer

It doesn't need to be a big one, but a freezer is an integral part of a kitchen in which healthy food is prepared and stored. If you want to cook ahead for an entire week, it's definitely best to have access to a freezer. Consider also freezing chopped fruit ready for your smoothies, slices of homemade bread, and fresh snacks.

Juicer

If you make a lot of juice, it's nice to own a good juicer. A blender produces a coarser blend, which is great for smoothies, but for a true juice you'll need either a slow juicer or a centrifugal juicer.

Scale

This is a must for anyone trying to get a handle on balanced eating, and for baking. I prefer to use a digital scale. They're easier to use and quite precise.

Food Processor

A good food processor does the heavy lifting, so to speak. Grinding, chopping, mixing. . . . A food processor is great for making spreads, sauces, processing dates, or making your own nut butters. Sometimes you can get away with using a blender for these things, but processing harder ingredients, such as nuts and dried fruit, is easiest in a food processor.

Spiralizer

This amazing appliance allows you to cut long, thin noodle-like strips from a variety of vegetables, including zucchini, carrots, and cucumber, in no time at all. Use one to make your salads more exciting and to prep vegetables as replacements for wheat products. I like to make "pasta" out of zucchini, for example. And carrot "noodles" instead of the real thing in soups.

Power Kitchen 2

*My little kitchen is full of **tools** and tasty **ingredients** because having good **supplies** is the foundation of healthy eating. That way you can just go out to grab the **fresh** ingredients you need and **get started**.*

Ghee

In addition to coconut oil, I also have clarified butter (ghee) in my fridge. You can heat it without releasing chemicals because certain milk products (such as casein and whey) are removed in the clarification process. This is why ghee is even acceptable for people with a dairy allergy or lactose intolerance. Make sure your ghee is made from butter produced by grass-fed cows.

Coconut Oil

I always choose *extra-virgin* coconut oil because it isn't overly processed, refined, or bleached. The oil is good for your immune system and has an antimicrobial effect. It also assists in balancing blood sugar. Coconut oil can be heated to high temperatures without losing its nutritional value or oxidizing.

Salt

When I mention salt in this book, what I am referring to is either *Celtic sea salt* or *Himalayan salt*. Himalayan salt is an unrefined land salt from the Himalayan mountains. Celtic sea salt is a product of sunlight and seawater. Both types of salt are high in minerals and trace elements.

Baking Soda

You can use this for just about anything. I brush my teeth with it, use it as a scrub, and clean my skin with it. I also use it to make my baked goods rise. Use baking soda only when there's an acidic ingredient in the recipe in question.

Veggie Powder Mix

This is a creation of mine (see page 137) that is a perfect replacement for a bouillon cube—free of crazy ingredients like yeast extract, MSG, soy, and corn protein. I always make a big jar full at one time so it lasts about a year. Short on time? Use a bouillon powder (cube) that is free of flavor enhancers and artificial flavors. Note: One teaspoon veggie powder mix is just about equal to one teaspoon bouillon powder.

Checklist
for Your Power Kitchen Cupboards

OILS AND FATS
- ✓ Coconut oil
- ✓ Ghee
- ✓ Olive oil, extra-virgin
- ✓ Rice oil

Flour
- ✓ Almond flour
- ✓ Coconut flour
- ✓ Oat flour
- ✓ Quinoa flour
- ✓ Whole-grain spelt flour

Grains and Seeds
- ✓ Chia seeds
- ✓ Fennel seeds
- ✓ Hemp seeds
- ✓ Lentils
- ✓ Millet
- ✓ Mustard seeds
- ✓ Oats
- ✓ Quinoa
- ✓ Quinoa flakes
- ✓ Rice paper sheets
- ✓ Sesame seeds
- ✓ Soba noodles
- ✓ Sunflower seeds

Dried Herbs
- ✓ Basil
- ✓ Celery salt
- ✓ Fennel
- ✓ Marjoram
- ✓ Oregano
- ✓ Parsley
- ✓ Red pepper flakes
- ✓ Rosemary
- ✓ Thyme

Sweets
- ✓ Cacao powder, raw
- ✓ Coconut sugar
- ✓ Figs
- ✓ Frozen fruit
- ✓ Honey, raw
- ✓ Maple syrup
- ✓ Medjool dates
- ✓ Raisins

Ground or Powdered Herbs and Spices
- ✓ Black pepper
- ✓ Cajun spice blend
- ✓ Cayenne pepper
- ✓ Cinnamon
- ✓ Cumin
- ✓ Curry powder
- ✓ Garam masala
- ✓ Garlic powder
- ✓ Laos powder
- ✓ Nutmeg
- ✓ Onion powder
- ✓ Salt
- ✓ Turmeric

Nuts
- ✓ Almonds
- ✓ Cashews
- ✓ Pecans
- ✓ Walnuts

Other
- ✓ Apple cider vinegar
- ✓ Baking soda
- ✓ Coconut milk
- ✓ Mustard
- ✓ Nori sheets
- ✓ Psyllium husks
- ✓ Tahini
- ✓ Tamari (wheat-free soy sauce)

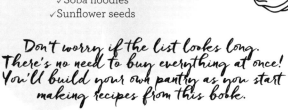

Don't worry if the list looks long. There's no need to buy everything at once! You'll build your own pantry as you start making recipes from this book.

Good to know

Flexitarian

If I eat animal products, I prefer poultry, wild fish, and goat's milk (or goat's milk cheese) because I've noticed my body tolerates these foods well. I believe in free-range and cruelty-free production. I like to buy animal products from a local producer or farmer that I trust. That way I always know where the products come from and that the animals in question were treated with respect. In this book, I always indicate when a recipe is vegetarian or vegan.

Gluten Free

Many of my recipes are gluten free. Gluten refers to a group of proteins contained in grains such as wheat, barley, rye, and spelt. I'm sensitive to gluten, as many people are. But there are also those who have an intolerance to gluten. In this book, I always indicate when a recipe is gluten free. Do be aware that certain grains that do not contain gluten (such as oats) may come in contact with gluten-containing grains during processing.

Tip: Vegan? Replace an egg in a recipe with this mixture: 1 egg = 1 tablespoon (11 g) chia seeds mixed with 6 tablespoons plus 2 teaspoons (100 ml) water. Combine and set aside for 15 minutes. You'll notice the mixture will thicken and come to resemble a gel or thick, egg-like pudding. Add this to the rest of the ingredients in the recipe.

Stuff

Lunch boxes are back! If you're all packed up and ready to go, it's a good idea to make sure your smoothies, salads, and snacks are contained in the right materials. You don't want your smoothie leaking into your bag—yes, this happened to me—or banana bread drying out before you can sink your teeth into it. It's also important to reduce the amount of waste we produce and avoid exposure to nasty chemicals in the products we use.

Sandwich Bags

Forget plastic! I use sandwich bags made of paper or cotton to transport a tasty slice of banana bread or a freshly made loaf. Your food will taste better coming out of this packaging and you can reuse the bags. Shaking the bags out is often enough to keep them clean, but there are also sandwich bags that can be washed.

Containers, Bottles, and Jars

If you're on the go often, it's really important to invest in tons of containers, bottles, and jars. How else are you supposed to take your fresh lunches, juices, and snacks with you on your way? You can also use these containers to store your creations in the refrigerator or freezer. The best choices are glass, stainless steel, or BPA (Bisphenol A)-free plastic that does not contain softeners or parabens.

Weck and Mason Jars

I use small hermetically sealing glass jars to store sauces and spreads or, because they seal so securely, to take with me on the go. I use larger jars as to-go containers for salads and smoothies. A mustard or jam jar works well and looks cool, too. Just remove the label—and voilà! Do make sure that any reused jars seal tightly.

Time Schedule

Timing is everything—also true when it comes to healthy eating. It's so often the case that you want to eat healthy, but that you just don't have the energy or time to perform miracles in the kitchen on a daily basis. Having a busy life means it's even more important to prepare as much as possible ahead of time. For each recipe in this book, I provide an indication of the time it takes to prepare it and when the best time is to make it.

Last Minute

These are the quick recipes that can be thrown together in no time flat. They include drinks, smoothies, and quick breakfasts. Though these recipes often taste best when freshly made, you can make a larger portion and store leftovers for the next day or two.

Sunday Prep

There are those days off (they don't have to be Sundays) that are perfect for spending in the kitchen. It's then that I take my sweet time in the kitchen, make a schedule for the week, do the grocery shopping, and start stockpiling . . . muffins, breads, spreads . . . anything that keeps for longer than three days. Doing this makes things so much easier during the week.

Day Before

These recipes are just a bit too time intensive for the morning of—or they need to sit for several hours or need to be cooked and fully cooled. In these instances, I tend to get to work the evening before. These recipes include breakfasts, soups, and salads. I also like to prep my lunch for the next day ahead of time and eat the same thing for dinner that night.

First things first

It's important to lay the foundation first. You've transformed your kitchen into a Power Kitchen, your cupboards are full of healthy ingredients, and you have the right stuff on hand to freeze and store and take with you. Now it's cooking time! I always keep a supply of granola on hand, bread in the freezer, cashew milk in the fridge, and chips, cookies, and snack balls in the cupboard. But all this requires a bit of patience. You can't lay the foundation in one day.

If you start cooking from this book on a regular basis, you'll build your own pantry automatically. You can also experiment on your own. A loaf of bread can last longer than a week, you can vary the snacks you make, or grab a piece of fruit or buy a healthy snack while you're out—every once in a while. And feel free to add your own recipes to your weekly schedule.

breakfast

Given the choice, I prefer to take my time in the morning, but even when I'm in a hurry, I make sure to eat a good (and, most importantly, tasty) breakfast. I can't eat that quickly, so I tend to just pack my brekkie and take it with me. Planning is key, so I often prep my breakfast in advance. That way you can avoid compromising on a nutritious start to the day and just focus on finding a quiet moment to enjoy your breakfast just about anywhere.

Choco-Buckwheat Porridge

Buckwheat is high in protein. Cacao makes you happy. Sounds like music to my ears! This breakfast has just the right vibes to start your day. It's delicious topped with a dollop of tahini and sliced banana.

PREPARATION TIME
7 minutes
SOAKING TIME
overnight
TOTAL TIME
overnight

INGREDIENTS
(serves 2)
* 5 ounces (140 g) buckwheat groats
* 6 Medjool dates, pitted
* 6 tablespoons plus 2 teaspoons (100 ml) plant-based milk
* 1 tablespoon raw cacao powder
* 1 teaspoon ground cinnamon
* ½ teaspoon ground cardamom
* ½ teaspoon unsweetened vanilla powder
* Pinch salt
* Tahini and banana slices, for garnish

KEEPS FOR
2 days in the fridge
SUPPLIES
blender; storage jars

DAY BEFORE

Method Soak the buckwheat groats in ample water overnight. The next morning, drain the buckwheat and transfer it to the blender. Add the dates and the remaining ingredients, *except* the tahini and banana. Blend until smooth. Too dry? Add a little bit of water to thin the mixture.

Spoon the porridge into a storage jar, top with the tahini and banana slices, and close the lid properly to create a seal so it doesn't leak into your bag as you head out the door.

Blueberry Muffins

These muffins make **breakfast** *a celebration. They are delicious,* **sweet,** *and, most importantly, so nutritious they give you the energy* **boost** *you need to* **start** *your day. Muffins are easily transported, so they're* **ideal** *for eating while* **on your way** *to, or sitting at, your* **desk.**

PREPARATION TIME
15 minutes
BAKING TIME
30 minutes
TOTAL TIME
45 minutes

INGREDIENTS
(makes 5 muffins)
* Coconut oil, for greasing
* 2 eggs
* 1 banana
* 6 tablespoons plus 2 teaspoons (100 ml) rice milk
* 1 tablespoon (15 ml) lemon juice
* 7 ounces (200 g) oat flour
* 2 teaspoons baking soda
* 1 teaspoon ground cinnamon
* 6 Medjool dates, pitted and chopped into small pieces
* 3½ ounces (100 g) frozen blueberries

KEEPS FOR
5 days in the fridge—you can also freeze them!

SUPPLIES
muffin tin

Method Preheat the oven to 350°F (180°C) and grease the muffin tin well.

Add the eggs, banana, rice milk, and lemon juice to the blender and process until frothy. Transfer the mixture to a mixing bowl and stir in the oat flour, baking soda, and cinnamon, stirring to combine until a thick batter forms.

Add the dates and blueberries to the batter. Stir well and divide the batter evenly among the muffin forms. Bake the muffins in the preheated oven for about 30 minutes. Let cool fully and enjoy these the whole week!

Ready. Prep.
Breakfast!

Pink Kick Start

It's the cranberries that make this brekkie so pretty in pink. If you find cranberries too sour, swap them for blackberries or add extra raisins or dates to up the sweetness factor. For breakfast, you may want to add some fresh raspberries on top.

PREPARATION TIME
15 minutes

INGREDIENTS
(2 to 3 servings)
* 5⅓ ounces (150 g) raw cashews
* 8½ fluid ounces (250 ml) coconut milk
* 7 ounces (200 g) frozen cranberries
* ½ cup plus 2 tablespoons (1¾ ounces, or 50 g) instant oatmeal or quinoa flakes
* 1¾ ounces (50 g) raisins
* 1 teaspoon unsweetened vanilla powder
* ½ teaspoon ground cardamom
* ½ teaspoon ground cinnamon
* Small handful fresh raspberries, for garnish

KEEPS FOR
1 day in the fridge

SUPPLIES
blender; 2 airtight containers

Method Soak the cashews in water for 10 minutes. Meanwhile, add the other ingredients to the blender. Add the drained cashews and blend until smooth. If it's not mixing well, add a bit of water. Divide the mixture into 2 containers. Take one with you and put the other in the fridge for the next day.

Tip: A handful of fresh raspberries on top of this brekkie really adds the finishing touch.

Medjool Dates

An ideal addition to sweet recipes. They are nice and big; the flesh is soft and every bite is sweet like honey.

Coffee

I like to make a nice big latte with oat milk and cinnamon in the morning, but I also use coffee in my muffins.

Cashews

Creamy and nutritious—I prefer to use the raw variety. I use them to make cream, milk, and nut butter and I also just eat them on their own as a snack.

Psyllium Husks

Derived from the seeds of the *Plantago ovata*, psyllium husks add firmness and elasticity to cakes, breads, and tarts. Perfect for gluten-free baking.

Vanilla Powder (unsweetened)

The seductress of the spices, sans sweetener. The smell of vanilla makes me happy and relaxed.

Oats (flour + whole oats)

I love the delicious, neutral flavor of oats. Breads, cakes, breakfasts: Adding oats guarantees softness and extra fiber.

Banana Mousse

The *flavors* of banana, strawberry, coconut, and *vanilla* create a calming *wake-up moment*—even when you're on the go. This *light* mousse can be whipped up in a matter of minutes in the *blender*. I usually make this the *night before* and make *two* servings at once.

PREPARATION TIME
5 minutes

INGREDIENTS
(2 servings)
* 1¾ ounces (50 g) coconut oil
* 2 Medjool dates, pitted
* 1 avocado, peeled, halved, and pitted
* 7 ounces (200 g) frozen strawberries
* 2 ripe bananas
* 1 teaspoon unsweetened vanilla powder

KEEPS FOR
2 days in the fridge

SUPPLIES
blender; 2 jars

Method Melt the coconut oil in a small saucepan, if necessary, and transfer it to the blender. Add the dates and avocado, as well as the remaining ingredients, to the blender. Process until smooth. Pour the mousse into 2 jars and refrigerate, uncovered, for 1 hour. Give the mousse a stir before eating.

Tip: Don't love the taste of coconut? Use refined coconut oil.

Breakfast Pancakes (photo pg. 16)

Pancakes for breakfast! Who says they're not a weekday breakfast? Cook them on a quiet evening and keep them in the fridge. In the morning, pile them in a to-go container, top them with a bit of fresh fruit, and voilà! A breakfast that can be eaten on the train or at the office that is sure to make your colleagues jealous.

PREPARATION TIME
20 minutes

DAY BEFORE

INGREDIENTS
(2 servings, or about 6 small pancakes)
* 2 bananas, peeled
* 1 mango (9 to 10½ ounces, or 250 to 300 g) cleaned, peeled, and pitted
* 1½ cups (4¼ ounces, or 120 g) instant oatmeal
* ½ teaspoon ground cinnamon
* Pinch salt
* Pinch unsweetened vanilla powder (optional)
* Coconut oil or ghee, for frying

KEEPS FOR
2 to 3 days in the fridge

SUPPLIES
blender or immersion blender; to-go container

Method Add the bananas and mango to the blender, along with the oatmeal, cinnamon, salt, and vanilla powder (if using). Blend until a smooth, thick batter forms. Transfer the batter to a bowl.

Meanwhile, melt 1 tablespoon (14 g) coconut oil in a frying pan over medium heat. Add 2 tablespoons (28 g) batter per pancake to the pan and press the pancakes down slightly. You should be able to cook 3 pancakes at a time. Flip the pancakes carefully and cook until golden brown on both sides. They should now be nice and crunchy. Add more coconut oil to the pan before you cook the next round of pancakes so they don't stick.

Nonstick Tip: If your pan does not have a nonstick coating, make your own with parchment paper. Cut a circle of parchment to fit the pan and cook the pancakes on top of it.

Granola *(photo pg. 125)*

Good old granola, but this time grain free. I usually make a big batch so I can keep taking a little bit to go in a container each day. I love granola with a homemade, plant-based milk. Bring a bottle of it with you in your bag and you've got a delicious breakfast or snack on hand that can be eaten virtually anywhere.

PREPARATION TIME
10 minutes
BAKING TIME
30 minutes
TOTAL TIME
40 minutes

SUNDAY PREP

INGREDIENTS
(makes about 15 ounces [425 g])
* 5⅓ ounces (150 g) almonds
* 1 cup (3½ ounces or 100 g) walnuts
* 2⅔ ounces (75 g) pecans
* 1 ounce (28 g) coconut oil
* 1 tablespoon (20 g) maple syrup or raw honey
* 2 teaspoons ground cinnamon
* Pinch salt
* 1½ ounces (45 g) dried blueberries or other dried fruit
* 1¾ ounces (50 g) coconut flakes

KEEPS FOR
1 month in an airtight container; 3 months in the freezer

SUPPLIES
clean tea towel; heavy ladle or rolling pin; baking sheet lined with parchment paper; Weck jar

Method Preheat the oven to 320°F (160°C). Place the almonds on the clean tea towel, fold it closed, and use the ladle or rolling pin to smash the almonds until quite fine. Add the other nuts and crush them as well.

Melt the coconut oil, if necessary, and combine it with all the other ingredients, *except* the blueberries and coconut flakes, in a large mixing bowl. Toss to combine and spread the mixture evenly across the parchment-lined baking sheet.

Place the granola in the middle of the preheated oven for 30 minutes, stirring every 10 minutes. During the last 5 minutes of cooking time (not earlier, they will brown too much), add the coconut flakes. Turn off the oven, open the oven door halfway, and let the granola cool fully in the oven. Once cool, mix in the blueberries and store in an airtight container.

Storage Tip: This granola stays good for up to three months when stored in the freezer. The trick is to store it in an airtight container, as full as possible. For the freshest granola in the morning, take a little bit out of the freezer the night before to thaw.

Have something to celebrate?
Serve the muffins on a tray
and top with homemade
chocolate sauce.

Chocolate Sauce
recipe pg. 130

Coffee Muffins

Sometimes there are those mornings when you don't even have time to make coffee... when just the smell of coffee makes you think of that much-needed moment of calm. What if you'd made these muffins ahead of time on your day off? They smell delicious.

PREPARATION TIME
20 minutes
BAKING TIME
40 minutes
TOTAL TIME
1 hour

INGREDIENTS
(makes 6 muffins)
* 3 tablespoons (33 g) chia seeds
* 7 ounces (200 g) Medjool dates, pitted
* 6 tablespoons plus 2 teaspoons (100 ml) brewed espresso
* 1 tablespoon (15 ml) fresh lemon juice
* 1 heaping tablespoon (14+ g) coconut oil, softened, plus more for greasing the muffin tin
* 5 ounces (140 g) oat flour or other flour of your choosing
* 2 teaspoons baking soda
* 1 teaspoon ground cinnamon
* 2 pinches unsweetened vanilla powder
* Pinch salt

KEEPS FOR
1 week in an airtight container
SUPPLIES
food processor; muffin tin; parchment paper

Method Preheat the oven to 350°F (180°C). Soak the chia seeds in 5 fluid ounces (150 ml) water. Blend the dates in the food processor until a soft mass forms. Combine the date purée with the chia seeds, espresso, lemon juice, and coconut oil in a large mixing bowl. Add the dry ingredients and stir well until a thick batter forms.

Grease the muffin tin with coconut oil. Fold a round or square piece of parchment paper for each muffin form and place it into the form. Spoon the batter into the parchment forms and bake in the preheated oven for about 40 minutes. Keep an eye on the muffins as they bake!

These muffins don't rise much, as the batter is quite heavy, but they are no less tasty because of it and actually more nutritious!

Every Day is
a Perfect Day
for a Picnic

Carrot Pancakes

Inspired by the classic carrot cake, I now make these carrot pancakes. They are actually tastiest eaten cold, so I often make a stack and keep them in the fridge. I top them with a bit of tahini syrup at home and take them with me to go.

PREPARATION TIME
30 minutes

INGREDIENTS
(makes 10 pancakes)
* 1 tablespoon chia seeds
* 4¾ ounces (135 g) carrots
* 1¾ ounces (50 g) walnuts
* 1 heaping tablespoon (14+ g) coconut oil
* 7¾ fluid ounces (230 ml) almond milk
* 5½ ounces (160 g) oat flour
* 1 tablespoon (15 ml) fresh lemon juice
* 2 teaspoons gingerbread spice mix
* ½ teaspoon baking soda
* Pinch salt
* Pinch unsweetened vanilla powder
* Tahini Syrup (page 131), for serving

KEEPS FOR
5 days in the fridge; or freeze them, divided into portions using parchment paper to separate them

SUPPLIES
food processor

SUNDAY PREP

Method Combine the chia seeds with 3 tablespoons plus 1 teaspoon (50 ml) water in a small bowl and set aside. Grate the carrots, finely chop the walnuts, and melt the coconut oil in a small saucepan, if necessary.

Once the chia seeds have absorbed the water, combine all the ingredients, *except* the tahini syrup, in a large mixing bowl. Let the mixture stand for about 10 minutes. Cook the pancakes without oil in a frying pan over high heat. Flip them after about 1½ minutes and cook the other side. Stack the cooked pancakes on top of each other and let cool. These pancakes are best kept in the fridge or frozen in portions. They're delicious with a bit of tahini syrup or just plain tahini.

*Tahini Syrup
recipe pg. 131*

Chocolate Sauce
recipe pg. 130

Next-Level Banana Split

Classic! Banana and chocolate sauce. And this version involves all the deliciousness and none of the guilt. I make this breakfast right before I run out the door, wrap it up in paper, and I'm ready to roll.

PREPARATION TIME
20 minutes

INGREDIENTS
(makes 1 roll)
* 1 egg
* 1 tablespoon (15 ml) oat milk
* Pinch gingerbread spice mix
* Pinch sea salt
* 1 tablespoon (14 g) coconut oil or ghee
* 1 banana
* 1 tablespoon (15 ml) Chocolate Sauce (page 130)

KEEPS FOR
1 day in the fridge

SUPPLIES
storage container; toothpick

Method Beat the egg until frothy, then stir in the oat milk, gingerbread spice mix, and sea salt. Heat a frying pan over medium heat. Melt the coconut oil in the pan and pour the mixture into the pan. Cook the mixture into an omelet and allow it to cool on a plate. Mash the banana and spoon it onto the middle of the omelet. Spoon a bit of chocolate sauce onto the omelet as well. Roll up the omelet, use a toothpick to secure it if you need to, and place it in a to-go container.

bread

Homemade bread is always a good idea.
You can try endless variations with nuts,
seeds, herbs, and different types of flour.
I love my recipes, but you can always create
your very own signature bread. I usually
bake two loaves of bread on a day off.
I freeze the sliced loaves right away so
I can just grab a couple of slices each day
to eat with a tasty spread or on the side
with a bowl of soup as breakfast or lunch.

Chocolate-Banana Bread

After a great deal of trial and error, it finally worked: the ultimate choco-banana bread recipe. It's perfectly moist, delicious as a snack, and even better as breakfast. I make sure to cut extra-thick slices and take them with me in a sandwich bag.

PREPARATION TIME
15 minutes
BAKING TIME
45 minutes
TOTAL TIME
1 hour

INGREDIENTS
(makes 1 loaf)
* ½ cup (4¼ ounces, or 120 g) coconut oil, melted, plus more for greasing the loaf pan
* 3 tablespoons (42 g) chia seeds
* 12⅓ ounces (350 g) peeled, ripe bananas
* ½ cup (120 ml) oat milk
1 tablespoon (15 ml) fresh lemon juice
* 5 Medjool dates, pitted
* 7 ounces (200 g) quinoa flour
* ¼ cup (22 g) raw cacao powder
* 2 teaspoons baking soda
* 1 teaspoon unsweetened vanilla powder
* 1 teaspoon salt

KEEPS FOR
about 5 days in an airtight container, or slice and freeze
SUPPLIES
small loaf pan (4 × 8 inches, or 10 × 20 cm); parchment paper

Method Preheat the oven to 350°F (180°C). Grease the loaf pan with coconut oil and line the bottom with parchment paper, greasing the paper as well. Soak the chia seeds for about 15 minutes in 5 fluid ounces (150 ml) water. Meanwhile, add the bananas, oat milk, melted coconut oil, lemon juice, and dates to the blender. Blend until well combined and creamy.

Combine the dry ingredients in a large mixing bowl. Add the wet ingredients to the dry ingredients and stir until fully combined. Add the soaked chia seeds to the mixture last and stir well. Transfer the batter to the greased loaf pan and place in the preheated oven for about 45 minutes, having a look every so often to check the bread's progress. When done, remove from the oven and let cool in the pan for 10 minutes. Remove from the pan and let cool fully on a wire rack.

Pecan Butter
recipe pg. 59

Cashew Butter
recipe pg. 59

Coconut Spice Bread

*The **combination** of **sweet potato**, coconut flavor, and gingerbread spices makes this bread truly **delicious** even without anything on it. Bake this bread on your **day off** so you can grab a **slice** throughout the week when you need something to take with you on the go. It's also great for **sharing**!*

PREPARATION TIME
30 minutes
BAKING TIME
40 minutes
TOTAL TIME
1 hour and 10 minutes

INGREDIENTS
(makes one loaf)
* 1 pound (450 g) sweet potatoes, peeled
* 4 medium-size eggs
* ¼ cup plus 1 teaspoon (about 2 ounces, or 60 g) coconut oil, melted, plus more for greasing the loaf pan
* ¼ cup (60 g) coconut yogurt
* 1 tablespoon (15 ml) fresh lemon juice
* 3¾ cups (10½ ounces, or 300 g) instant oatmeal
* 1 tablespoon baking soda
* 2 teaspoons gingerbread spice mix
* 1 teaspoon unsweetened vanilla powder
* Pinch salt

KEEPS FOR
5 days in the fridge
SUPPLIES
food processor or blender; loaf pan (10 inch, or 25 cm)

Method Chop the sweet potatoes into equal-size pieces. Boil for 10 to 15 minutes until cooked. Let cool, and preheat the oven to 350°F (180°C).

Transfer the cooked sweet potatoes to the food processor or blender along with the eggs, coconut oil, yogurt, and lemon juice and blitz until frothy. Combine the dry ingredients in a large mixing bowl, stirring well to combine. Add the wet ingredients to the dry ingredients and combine fully. Grease the loaf pan with coconut oil, transfer the batter to the pan, and place in the preheated oven for about 40 minutes, checking on the bread every so often.

Remove the bread from the oven and let cool in the pan for 10 minutes and then out of the pan, directly on a wire rack, until fully cooled.

Nothing
to hide,
just goodness
inside

Lentil Tapenade
recipe pg. 58

Fennel Loaf

Herbs and nuts can add a twist to any bread recipe. In this fennel loaf, I use deliciously aromatic fennel seeds. I love their soft, anise-like flavor! This loaf is great with a savory tapenade.

PREPARATION TIME
10 minutes
BAKING TIME
30 to 35 minutes
TOTAL TIME
about 45 minutes

INGREDIENTS
(makes one loaf)
* 3 eggs
* 2 tablespoons (30 ml) fresh lemon juice
* 6 tablespoons plus 2 teaspoons (100 ml) oat milk or water
* ½ cup plus 2 tablespoons (about 2 ounces, or 60 g) almond flour
* 7 tablespoons plus 1½ teaspoons (80 g) buckwheat flour
* 1½ ounces (40 g) psyllium husks
* 2 tablespoons (22 g) chia seeds
* 1 tablespoon baking soda
* 1½ teaspoons fennel seeds
* 2 small handfuls walnuts, finely chopped (optional)
* 2 tablespoons (28 g) coconut oil, melted, plus more for greasing the pan

KEEPS FOR
5 days in the fridge, or freeze
SUPPLIES
small loaf pan (4 × 8 inches, or 10 × 20 cm); toothpick

DAY BEFORE

Method Preheat the oven to 350°F (180°C). Beat the eggs in a bowl until fluffy. Add the lemon juice and oat milk (or other plant-based milk) to the eggs and whisk to combine. Next, add the dry ingredients. Add the walnuts (if using) and the coconut oil. Stir well to combine. Grease the loaf pan with coconut oil and pour in the batter. Bake in the preheated oven for 30 to 35 minutes.

Have a look at the bread toward the end of the cooking time and check for doneness using a toothpick: Pierce the middle of the loaf with the toothpick, if it comes out clean the bread is done! Let the bread cool, remove it from the pan, and slice. It's delicious with lentil spread and a splash of olive oil.

Broccoli Sandwich

When I was in New York recently, I ordered a sandwich made of…
broccoli. And when I got home, I felt compelled to try to make this myself.
Take a couple (or more) slices with you for lunch. Bring your toppings or
spreads, like hummus, lettuce, tomato, cucumber, and a bit of Homemade
Mayonnaise (page 134), with you in separate containers.

PREPARATION TIME
10 minutes
BAKING TIME
30 minutes
TOTAL TIME
40 minutes

INGREDIENTS
(makes 18 slices)
* 1 pounds (450 g) broccoli
florets, removed from the stems
* 3 eggs
* 1¼ cups (5⅓ ounces, or 150 g)
oat flour or other flour of choice
* ⅓ cup (1¾ ounces, or 50 g)
goat cheese, grated
* 1 tablespoon psyllium husks
* ½ teaspoon freshly
ground black pepper
* Salt, to taste

KEEPS FOR
5 days in the fridge in an
airtight container
SUPPLIES
food processor; parchment
paper; rolling pin

Method Preheat the oven to 350°F (180°C). Place the
broccoli florets in the food processor and process
until finely ground. Beat the eggs in a large mixing
bowl until fluffy and add the remaining ingredients.
Knead into a large ball of dough. Line a baking sheet
with parchment paper. Spread the dough out on the
baking sheet, lay another sheet of parchment paper
on top, and use the rolling pin to roll out the dough
until it is about ⅓ inch (8 mm) thick.

Slice the rolled dough into rectangles and place the
baking sheet in the preheated oven. Bake for 30
minutes, or until the edges begin to brown.

*Tip: Usually toss the broccoli stalks? Stop! All the
vitamins in the florets are also found in the stalk.
Delicious in a salad or with other vegetables cooked
in a wok.*

Avocado Soup
recipe pg. 79

Cauliflower Buns

*I bake these **petits pains** on my day off so I can take them with me throughout the **week**. You can top them just as you would any **bun**. My favorite combo? Hard goat cheese, steamed **mackerel**, cherry tomatoes, **chives**, Homemade Mayonnaise (page 134), and pepper.*

PREPARATION TIME
10 minutes
BAKING TIME
35 minutes
TOTAL TIME
45 minutes

INGREDIENTS
(makes 5 or 6 buns)
* 1 medium-size (1 pound, or 450 g) head cauliflower
* 2 eggs
* 3½ ounces (100 g) oat flour
* 1 teaspoon ground cumin
* ½ teaspoon salt

KEEPS FOR
5 days in the fridge in an airtight container

SUPPLIES
baking sheet; food processor; parchment paper

Method Preheat the oven to 400°F (200°C) and line the baking sheet with parchment paper.

Clean the cauliflower and remove the florets. Process the florets in the food processor until they have the consistency of rice, but don't process them so much that they become watery. Beat the eggs until fluffy and combine them with the cauliflower and the other ingredients in a large mixing bowl. Stir well to combine. Form the dough into 5 or 6 balls and place them on the parchment-lined baking sheet. Bake the buns in the preheated oven for 35 minutes, remove from the oven, and let cool. Slice the buns through the middle and top them any way you'd like.

Millet
Use this gluten-free grain in breakfasts, in salads, or to "bread" fish.

Honey
I prefer raw, unprocessed, unpasteurized honey directly from the beekeeper. So sweet!

Coconut yogurt
No dairy, no sugar, no soy, or other additives. It's great with granola or added when baking to up the creaminess.

Figs

Dried as a snack, baked into bread, or chopped and added to muesli. I also eat them fresh, added to my fruit salad, when they're in season.

Cauliflower

A golden oldie that I only recently rediscovered. I make pizzas, salads, and even buns out of it.

Tamari

Wheat-free soy sauce with a sharper flavor and strong aroma. Tasty in dips, dressings, and soups.

Fruity Bread

Do you have a *sweet tooth*? Then this is the bread for *you*! It's really filling, so one *thick slice* is enough. It's delicious with *nut butter*, but it's truly indulgent with chocolate spread or *chia jam*.

PREPARATION TIME
10 minutes
BAKING TIME
50 minutes
TOTAL TIME
1 hour

INGREDIENTS
(makes 1 loaf)
* 3 tablespoons (33 g) chia seeds
* 3½ ounces (100 g) dried figs, chopped into small pieces
* 2 cups minus 2 tablespoons (5⅓ ounces, or 150 g) instant oatmeal
* 4¼ ounces (120 g) sunflower seeds
* 1 ounce (28 g) psyllium husks
* 1 teaspoon ground cinnamon
* 1 teaspoon baking soda
* Pinch unsweetened vanilla powder
* 5½ ounces (160 g) applesauce
* 2½ ounces (70 g) raisins
* 1 tablespoon (14 g) coconut oil, softened, plus more for greasing the pan

KEEPS FOR
5 days in a dry, airtight container; can also be frozen

SUPPLIES
loaf pan (8 × 5 inches, or 13 × 20 cm)

Method Preheat the oven to 350°F (180°C). Soak the chia seeds for 15 minutes in 5 fluid ounces (150 ml) water. Combine the figs with the dry ingredients and stir well to combine. Add the applesauce, raisins, coconut oil, and soaked chia seeds and stir again until fully combined. Grease the loaf pan with coconut oil, transfer the dough to the pan, and place in the preheated oven for about 50 minutes. Have a look every now and then to make sure the bread does not burn. To test for doneness, insert a toothpick into the center of the loaf; if it comes out clean it is done. The loaf might look a bit wet when it comes out of the pan, but the moisture will be absorbed, in large part, during the cooling process.

Tip: While you're at it, double the recipe and make two loaves and freeze one. That way you'll always have a breakfast, lunch, or snack on hand when you're too busy to make anything else.

On Top

The right **topping** *can make homemade bread even better. Lentils, pecans,* **cashews** *... with* **tapenades** *and nut butters, the* **sky's the limit.** *Make an extra* **big batch** *on your day off so you can use it,* **bit by bit,** *all week long. And* **sometimes** *... I just can't resist dipping my* **finger** *directly into the jar. That's* **allowed.***

3X SUNDAY PREP

Lentil Tapenade

PREPARATION TIME
20 minutes, plus 10 minutes
if you need to cook your lentils.

INGREDIENTS
*(makes about 1 pound,
5 ounces [600 grams])*
* 9 ounces (250 g) cooked beluga lentils
(about 4½ ounces, or 125 g dried)
* 3½ ounces (100 g) sundried tomatoes
* 6 tablespoons (90 ml)
extra-virgin olive oil
* 1 clove garlic
* 1 medium-size onion, finely chopped
* 5⅓ ounces (150 g) tomato paste
* Small handful fresh
flat-leaf parsley leaves
* 2 teaspoons ground cumin
* 1½ teaspoons apple cider vinegar
* 1 teaspoon paprika
* ½ teaspoon freshly
ground black pepper

KEEPS FOR
1 week in the fridge

SUPPLIES
food processor; 1 or 2 Weck jars

Method If cooking the lentils, place the dried lentils in a sieve, rinse thoroughly with cold water, and drain completely. Simmer the lentils in twice as much water as lentils for 20 to 30 minutes until cooked (or follow the package instructions). Drain the cooked lentils in a sieve, rinsing briefly with cold water. Let cool fully. Meanwhile, add the sundried tomatoes, olive oil, and garlic to the food processor and pulse to chop finely. Transfer the tomato mixture to a mixing bowl and add the onion and the remaining ingredients. Stir well to combine. Store the tapenade in nice Weck jars so they are easy to transport. This is delicious on the fennel loaf as a lunchtime sandwich.

I always use raw pecan nuts to make this, but you can also roast them in the oven for 10 minutes beforehand if you prefer.

Pecan Butter

PREPARATION TIME
15 minutes

INGREDIENTS
(makes 10½ ounces [300 g])
* 10½ ounces (300 g) pecans
* 1 tablespoon (15 ml) hazelnut oil or coconut oil (optional)
* ½ teaspoon unsweetened vanilla powder
* Pinch salt

KEEPS FOR
at least 2 to 3 months

SUPPLIES
food processor; small jar with tight-fitting lid

Method Add all the ingredients to the food processor and blitz until finely ground. This usually takes 5 to 10 minutes, in which time you'll notice the nuts go through various phases. They will change from coarse grains to finely ground meal and then, as they begin to release their oil, they become a creamy nut butter. Keep processing the nuts until the nut butter becomes fluid and creamy.

Transfer the nut butter to a small jar. This nut butter keeps for a very long time, but I don't think it'll take long before the jar is empty. Delicious!

Cashew Butter

PREPARATION TIME
10 minutes

INGREDIENTS
(makes 1 pound [450 g])
* 1 pound (450 g) raw cashews
* ½ teaspoon unsweetened vanilla powder
* Pinch salt

KEEPS FOR
3 months in an airtight container

SUPPLIES
food processor; 2 small jars, or 1 large jar, with tight-fitting lids

Method Add all the ingredients to the food processor and blitz until finely ground. This usually takes 5 to 10 minutes. Keep processing the nuts until they begin to release their oils and the mixture becomes fluid and creamy. Transfer the nut butter to the jar(s). Mmm, tasty!

lunch

People often look at me with envy. . . . What do you have in your lunch now? And I will admit, my lunches do tend to look a little more spectacular than your average cheese sandwich. I usually make my lunches the evening before. It saves time and guarantees I eat nutritious food during busy days. The lunch recipes in this book can also be eaten as dinner. I'll often make a salad for dinner, for example, and take the leftovers with me for lunch the next day.

Fennel Loaf
recipe pg. 49

Beet Soup in a Jar

This is really a **gazpacho** *made with beets. This soup is served* **cold,** *so it's* **perfect** *for taking with you in a* **jar** *or bottle—just don't forget your* **spoon!** *The best way to eat it, though, is with a slice of* **Fennel Loaf** *(page 49).*

PREPARATION TIME
30 minutes

INGREDIENTS
(serves 2 [makes about 1 quart, or 1 liter])
* 5 raw beets (a little more than 1 pound, or 500 g total), rinsed well
* 1 apple
* 1 small onion
* 1 clove garlic
* 2 teaspoons Veggie Powder Mix (page 137)
* 1 small handful fresh oregano leaves
* 1 teaspoon ground cinnamon
* Pinch salt
* About 2 tablespoons (⅔ ounce, or 18.75 g) fresh goat cheese or a small handful of feta cheese

KEEPS FOR
2 to 3 days in the fridge

SUPPLIES
blender; 2 jars or bottles (16 fluid ounces, or 500 ml) with tight-fitting lids

Method You don't need to peel the beets, just leave them whole. Boil them in abundant water for about 20 minutes, or until fully cooked. Test for doneness by inserting a thin knife into the beets. If the knife slides out easily the beets are cooked. Drain the beets, let cool, and chop them into small pieces.

Clean and chop the apple, onion, and garlic and transfer them to the blender. Add 27 fluid ounces (800 ml) water, the veggie powder mix, oregano, cinnamon, salt, and the cooked beets to the blender as well. Process into a smooth soup and pour the soup into 2 jars or bottles and stir the goat cheese into each one (or sprinkle with feta).

You can eat this soup warm, of course. Just transfer the soup from the blender to a saucepan and heat it on low. Just don't let it boil, as boiling destroys some of the nutrients this soup naturally contains.

Sauerkraut Tart

*Sauerkraut, or **fermented** cabbage, is **hyper** healthy. And it's not only something you serve with mashed potatoes—you can make a **tart** out of it! **Make** this ahead of time, on the **weekend**, so you can grab a **big** slice for **lunch** during the week. It'll keep you feeling sour . . . (I mean **sweet**!) all **week** long.*

PREPARATION TIME
20 minutes
BAKING TIME
35 minutes
TOTAL TIME
just under 1 hour

SUNDAY PREP

INGREDIENTS
(makes 1 tart)
* 3½ ounces (100 g) raisins
* 2¼ pounds (1 kg) sweet potatoes, peeled and chopped into equal-size pieces
* 1 medium-size onion, finely chopped
* Coconut oil or ghee, for frying and greasing the pan
* 3 eggs
* 14 ounces (400 g) sauerkraut, drained
* 7 ounces (200 g) oat flour
* Small handful fresh thyme leaves, finely chopped
* Freshly ground black pepper, to taste
* 5⅓ ounces (150 g) feta cheese
* 2 to 3 tablespoons (18 to 27 g) sunflower seeds

KEEPS FOR
4 days in the fridge; can also be frozen
SUPPLIES
tart or quiche pan (11 inches, or 28 cm), greased

Method Soak the raisins in a bowl of boiling water for about 15 minutes. Boil the sweet potatoes in ample water for about 15 minutes, or until fully cooked. Drain and let cool. Meanwhile, sauté the onion with a spoonful of coconut oil in a frying pan until translucent.

Preheat the oven to 350°F (180°C). Beat the eggs until fluffy in a large mixing bowl. Mash the cooked sweet potatoes. Drain the raisins. In the bowl with the beaten eggs, combine the raisins, mashed sweet potatoes, sauerkraut, oat flour, onion, thyme, and pepper. Crumble half the feta into the bowl and stir well to combine. Transfer to the greased tart pan and crumble the rest of the feta over the top. Sprinkle with sunflower seeds and place in the preheated oven for about 35 minutes.

Tip: Also delicious with smoked salmon added for extra protein!

You can slice the tart into pieces and freeze them.

Stains?
I don't care.
A kitchen princess
doesn't need to be
a fashion queen!

Mint-Pomegranate Salad

Pomegranate = *power fruit*. The seeds are *deliciously* sweet and *sour*, full of *antioxidants* and vitamins, and are *even known* to be an *aphrodisiac* ... ooh la la! The *combination* here with *mint leaves* makes this the perfect *light* lunch on a *warm* day.

PREPARATION TIME
30 minutes plus cooling

INGREDIENTS
(serves 2 to 3)
* 4¼ ounces (120 g) millet
* 1 teaspoon Veggie Powder Mix (page 137)
* Scant 4 cups (2⅔ ounces, or 75 g) arugula
* 1 pomegranate, halved, seeds removed (see Tip)
* About 1½ tablespoons (⅓ ounce, or 10 g) fresh mint leaves, finely chopped
* Small handful roasted almonds
* ½ teaspoon freshly ground black pepper
* Cashew Dressing (page 131)

KEEPS FOR
2 days in the fridge

SUPPLIES
fine-mesh sieve

Method Rinse the millet in a fine-mesh sieve and drain completely. Bring 10 fluid ounces (300 ml) water to a boil in a large pan. Add the millet and simmer for 20 minutes until al dente. Drain the cooked millet using the sieve and transfer to a large bowl. Stir in the veggie powder mix and let cool. Combine all the ingredients in a to-go container, *except* the dressing, and refrigerate. Pour a bit of the cashew dressing into a separate jar to take with.

Tip: Give the pomegranate's skin a good whack using a ladle before slicing it in half. This helps loosen the seeds.

*Cashew Dressing
recipe pg. 131*

Mini Frittatas
recipe pg. 78

Celeriac Soup

This *flavorful* soup is ready in **no time**. I will usually have this soup for **dinner** and take the **leftovers** with me for lunch the next day. This soup is even **better** cold, so it's **ideal** for taking on the **go**!

PREPARATION TIME
30 minutes

INGREDIENTS
(serves 3 to 4)
* Coconut oil or ghee, for frying
* 1 medium-size onion, finely chopped
* 2 cloves garlic, finely chopped
* 17½ ounces (500 g) celeriac, peeled and finely chopped
* 2 teaspoons Veggie Powder Mix (page 137)
* 15 fluid ounces (450 ml) coconut milk
* 9 ounces (250 g) sweet potatoes, scrubbed clean and finely chopped
* Salt and freshly ground black pepper, to taste
* Pinch ground cardamom
* 7 ounces (200 g) mushrooms, finely chopped
* 1¾ ounces (50 g) sundried tomatoes
* 3 tablespoons (9 g) finely chopped fresh chives, plus more for garnish
* Tamari (optional)

KEEPS FOR
a maximum of 3 days in the fridge

SUPPLIES
blender

DAY BEFORE

Method Melt some coconut oil in a large pan. Sauté the onion until glassy, adding the garlic and celeriac after about 1 minute. Gently sauté the mixture for 10 minutes.

Stir in 25 fluid ounces (750 ml) water, the veggie powder mix, coconut milk, sweet potatoes, and herbs. Bring to a boil and simmer for about 15 minutes until the vegetables are cooked.

Meanwhile, sauté the mushrooms in a spoonful of coconut oil in a small frying pan.

Transfer the soup to a blender, add the sundried tomatoes, blend, and pour into bowls. Garnish the soup with the sautéed mushrooms and sprinkle with the chives. Season to taste with tamari (if using).

Cauliflower Couscous

You *taste* couscous, but you're eating . . . cauliflower? By using *vegetables* in place of *grains*, you'll keep this dish light, but it'll still give you the same *boost*. The secret to this recipe? A *night* in the fridge makes this dish taste even *better*.

PREPARATION TIME
30 minutes

INGREDIENTS
(serves 2)
* 10½ ounces (300 g) chicken breast
* 1 teaspoon curry powder
* Salt and freshly ground black pepper, to taste
* 1 large head cauliflower
* Coconut oil or ghee, for frying
* 1 medium-size onion, finely chopped
* 2 cloves garlic, finely chopped
* 1 bell pepper, any color, finely chopped
* 7 ounces (200 g) mixed mushrooms, finely chopped
* 1 teaspoon ground ginger
* 1½ teaspoons Red Curry Paste (page 136)
* 2 teaspoons tamari
* 2 eggs
* Large handful fresh baby spinach
* Small handful roasted almonds
* Bit of feta cheese (optional)

KEEPS FOR
2 days in the fridge

SUPPLIES
food processor; large wok

DAY BEFORE

Method Slice the chicken breast into cubes or strips and toss them in the curry powder and a bit of salt and pepper. Remove the cauliflower stalk and transfer the florets to the food processor. Process for about 30 seconds until the cauliflower has the texture of rice. Don't process too long—the cauliflower should be fluffy, not soupy.

Heat a bit of coconut oil in the wok. Sauté the onion, adding the garlic after about 1 minute. Then add the chicken, sauté for 1 minute, and add the bell pepper, mushrooms, ginger, curry paste, and tamari. Toss to combine and continue cooking until the chicken is done.

Add the cauliflower and sauté with the other ingredients for a couple of minutes. Make a well in the cauliflower couscous and break the eggs into the well. Stir the eggs into the couscous until they have solidified. Finally, add the spinach. Remove from the heat, sprinkle with the almonds, and crumble a bit of feta over top (if using). Done and done!

Tip: Would you rather make this a vegetarian dish? Just replace the chicken with feta.

I always make a list before I go to the grocery store. Sometimes I even remember to bring it with me.

Summer Quiche

The great thing about quiche is you can experiment with it endlessly. You can throw in whatever you have lying around and a single quiche will get you through several days. I went a bit crazy with greens in this summer version and made it ultra-light sans crust.

PREPARATION TIME
10 minutes
BAKING TIME
30 to 35 minutes
TOTAL TIME
about 40 minutes

INGREDIENTS
(makes 1 quiche)
* Coconut oil or ghee, for greasing the dish
* ⅓ cup (1¾ ounces, or 50 g) fresh or frozen peas
* 5 eggs
* 4 cups (4¼ ounces, or 120 g) fresh spinach, roughly chopped
* 3½ ounces (100 g) quinoa flakes or whole oats
* 1 large onion, finely chopped
* 2 cloves garlic, finely chopped
* Small handful fresh thyme leaves, finely chopped, or 1 teaspoon dried
* Small handful fresh oregano leaves, finely chopped, or 1 teaspoon dried
* 1 teaspoon tamari
* Pinch salt
* Pinch freshly ground black pepper
* About 4½ ounces (125 g) soft goat cheese

KEEPS FOR
3 days in the fridge
SUPPLIES
small round ovenproof dish
(8 inches, or 20 cm), greased

DAY BEFORE

Method Preheat the oven to 350°F (180°C). Boil the peas for 2 minutes, transfer to a sieve, and rinse with cold water. Drain completely. Beat the eggs in a large bowl and add all the ingredients, *except* the goat cheese. Stir well and pour into the prepared baking dish. Place dollops of goat cheese on top. Place the dish in the preheated oven and bake for 30 to 35 minutes.

Mini Frittatas *photo pg. 70*

*For the past little **while**, I've been making frittatas with whatever **leftovers** I happen to have on hand, but, to be **honest**, I like these **mini-versions** so much more. And because they're so **petit**, it's **easy** to take them with you in your **lunch box**.*

PREPARATION TIME
10 minutes
BAKING TIME
30 minutes
TOTAL TIME
40 minutes

SUNDAY PREP

INGREDIENTS
(makes 6 mini frittatas)
* 1 clove garlic, finely chopped
* 1 small onion, finely chopped
* Coconut oil or ghee, for frying
* 6 eggs
* 1 teaspoon freshly ground black pepper
* ½ teaspoon ground cumin
* ½ teaspoon salt
* About ⅓ cup (⁷⁄₁₀ ounce, or 20 g) kale, rinsed and chopped
* 1½ ounces (40 g) feta cheese
* Red pepper flakes, to taste (optional)

KEEPS FOR
1 week in the fridge
SUPPLIES
muffin tin with at least 6 forms

Method Preheat the oven to 350°F (180°C). Sauté the garlic and onion for a few minutes in a frying pan with a bit of coconut oil.

Whisk the eggs until fluffy. Stir in the pepper, cumin, and salt. Divide the kale across the 6 muffin forms. Add some of the feta and sautéed onion and garlic to each form. Top with the beaten eggs. Sprinkle each mini frittata with red pepper flakes (if using). Place the frittatas in the preheated oven and bake for 30 minutes. Enjoy these delicious items for 6 days. Tasty with a salad or soup for lunch.

Avocado Soup *photo pg. 52*

Thanks to the avocado, this dish packs more **healthy** *fats and* **nutrients** *than your average* **soup***. Pour it into two jars, take one with you, and* **keep** *the other in the fridge for another day.* **Delicious** *with a slice of bread or* **crackers** *for dipping.*

PREPARATION TIME
15 minutes

INGREDIENTS
(makes about 1 quart [1 liter])
* ½ lime
* Splash extra-virgin olive oil
* 3 avocados, peeled and pitted
* ½ cucumber
* 1 clove garlic
* 4 teaspoons (about 12 g) Veggie Powder Mix (page 137)
* Small handful fresh baby spinach
* Small handful fresh cilantro leaves
* 1 tablespoon fresh thyme leaves
* 1 teaspoon salt
* ½ teaspoon Cajun spices
* Pinch freshly ground black pepper
* Pinch ground cumin
* 4 vine-ripened tomatoes
* ½ cup (75 g) feta cheese

KEEPS FOR
2 days in the fridge
SUPPLIES
blender; 2 jars (16 fluid ounces, or 475 ml) with tight-fitting lids

LAST MINUTE

Method Squeeze the lime into the blender and add the remaining ingredients—*except* the tomatoes and feta—along with 10 fluid ounces (300 ml) water. Purée until creamy.

Pour into the 2 jars. Slice the tomatoes into small pieces and sprinkle over each portion of soup. Crumble some feta into each jar as well. Enjoy!

Tip: Don't love cilantro? Try fresh flat-leaf parsley.

Almond Sauce
recipe pg. 130

Gado Gado

This one is for my sweetest Indonesian friend. Voilà! A mix-mix dish with a surprising twist. Take it with you in a to-go container, sauce packed separately, a quarter lime on the side. . . . A delicious, healthy lunch just about anywhere. Guaranteed.

PREPARATION TIME
about 45 minutes

INGREDIENTS
(serves 2)
* Coconut oil or ghee, for frying
* 1 (10½-ounce, or 300 g) chicken breast
* About ⅔ cup (4¼ ounces, or 120 g) brown rice (I prefer basmati)
* 1 teaspoon Veggie Powder Mix (page 137)
* 9 ounces (250 g) green beans
* 7 ounces (200 g) red cabbage
* ½ cucumber
* 5⅓ ounces (150 g) shiitake mushrooms
* ¼ head napa cabbage
* Large handful bean sprouts
* 1 large carrot (7 ounces, or 200 g)
* 1 lime, quartered
* Almond Sauce (page 130)

KEEPS FOR
2 days in the fridge

SUPPLIES
spiralizer or vegetable peeler

Method Heat the coconut oil in a frying pan over low heat and cook the chicken breast, whole. Once cooked, pull the chicken meat apart using two forks and set it aside. Cook the brown rice according to the package directions, drain, and stir in the veggie powder mix. Clean all the vegetables. Boil the green beans for about 10 minutes, drain, rinse with cold water, and drain again. Slice the red cabbage, napa cabbage, cucumber, and shiitakes into thin strips. Sauté the shiitakes for 2 minutes on high heat in a bit of coconut oil. Slice the carrot using the spiralizer. Divide the vegetables between 2 to-go containers, placing the lime quarters on the side. Take the almond sauce with you in a separate container.

Tip: Would you prefer this to be vegetarian? Replace the chicken with a hard-boiled egg.

Rainbow Noodle Salad *with Almond Dressing*

Color = healthy—at least when it's natural. This salad is a color explosion on your plate and a vitamin explosion for your body. I discovered this salad in Australia and I'm reminded of that inspiring trip every time I make it.

PREPARATION TIME
25 minutes

INGREDIENTS
(serves 2)
* 3½ ounces (100 g) rice noodles, preferably brown
* About 1½ tablespoons (⅓ ounce, or 10 g) fresh mint leaves
* 1 small red onion
* 4¼ ounces (120 g) shiitake mushrooms or brown mushrooms
* 1 yellow bell pepper
* Coconut oil or ghee, for frying
* 1 large carrot
* 1 avocado
* Small handful bean sprouts
* 2 cups (about 2 ounces, or 60 g) fresh baby spinach
* 1 tablespoon (8 g) sesame seeds
* Almond Dressing (page 130)
* 1 lime, for sprinkling on the salad

KEEPS FOR
2 days in the fridge
SUPPLIES
colander; spiralizer or vegetable peeler

Method Bring a large pot of water to a boil. Add the rice noodles, pushing them into the pot until submerged. Return to a boil and cook for 5 to 6 minutes. Transfer to a colander, rinse with cold water, and drain fully.

Meanwhile, clean the vegetables and finely chop the mint, red onion, shiitakes, and bell pepper. Sauté the shiitakes for 2 minutes in a bit of coconut oil in a frying pan, remove from the heat, and let cool. Slice the carrot using the spiralizer.

Arrange the cooked noodles and all the vegetables in neat, color-specific rows in a to-go container and sprinkle with sesame seeds. Store the almond dressing separately, with the lime. Dress the salad just before you eat it and squeeze a little lime juice over top.

*Almond Dressing
recipe pg. 130*

Egg

An egg from the local farm is the tastiest, of course, but when this isn't an option I choose eggs from chickens I know have been treated well.

Shiitake

A spicy mushroom that consists primarily of water, protein, and carbohydrates. This variety is available year-round.

Sauerkraut

Full of healthy bacteria, which keeps your intestinal flora happy. This fermented vegetable is great served with a sweet sauce or baked into a tart.

Maple syrup

In addition to dates, this is one of my favorite sweeteners. It comes naturally from the maple tree, and its caramel flavor makes it the perfect addition to cookies or a topping for pancakes.

Snap peas

So deliciously crunchy when cooked in a wok or blanched. A tasty, fresh addition to a salad or noodle dish.

Salmon-Quinoa Salad

This salad is full of good fats and protein and is an ideal pre- or post-workout meal. It's also fantastic on a busy workday when you need an extra energy boost. The fish herb mix is homemade, too. I usually make one big batch of it at a time.

PREPARATION TIME
40 minutes

INGREDIENTS
(serves 2 to 3)
* 4¼ ounces (120 g) quinoa
* 10½ ounces (300 g) wild salmon fillet, cubed
* 2 teaspoons Fish Herb Mix (page 137)
* 2 teaspoons coconut oil, plus more, melted, for marinating the salmon
* 7 ounces (200 g) mushrooms
* 3 vine-ripened tomatoes
* 5⅓ ounces (150 g) snap peas
* 1 zucchini
* Small handful fresh basil leaves
* Nut Dressing (page 131)

KEEPS FOR
2 days in the fridge
SUPPLIES
spiralizer or vegetable peeler; jar with a tight-fitting lid

DAY BEFORE

Method Rinse the quinoa well, cook it according to the package directions, drain, and let cool. Marinate the salmon cubes in the fish herb mix and a bit of melted coconut oil. Meanwhile, clean the vegetables and finely chop the mushrooms and tomatoes. Melt the coconut oil in a frying pan and cook the salmon fully. Add the chopped vegetables and snap peas and sauté alongside the salmon, stirring occasionally. Let cool.

Slice the zucchini using the spiralizer. Place everything in the fridge. The next day, place the salad in the jar, in layers, top with a bit of basil, and take the dressing with you on the side.

Nut Dressing
recipe pg. 131

Drink Your Veggies
recipe pg. 126

The Best Dip Ever
recipe pg. 131

Spring Rolls with Chicken and The Best Dip Ever

With these rolls, the old adage—practice makes perfect—really does apply. Once you get good at making these, you'll have a fantastic-looking lunch, two days in a row. Take the dip with you in a separate container (with a tight-fitting lid!).

PREPARATION TIME
40 minutes

INGREDIENTS
(makes 6 spring rolls)
* 6 napa cabbage leaves or iceberg lettuce leaves
* 1 tablespoon (14 g) coconut oil
* 1 (14-ounce, or 400 g) chicken breast
* 1 clove garlic, minced
* 1 teaspoon tamari
* 6 edible rice paper sheets
* 1 teaspoon fresh mint leaves, finely chopped
* 1⅓ cups (20 g) fresh cilantro leaves
* 3½ ounces (100 g) red bell pepper, sliced into thin strips
* 4¼ ounces (120 g) carrot, sliced into thin strips
* 3½ ounces (100 g) cucumber, sliced into thin strips
* 1 tablespoon (8 g) sesame seeds
* The Best Dip Ever (page 131)

KEEPS FOR
2 days in the fridge
SUPPLIES
paper towels;
clean tea towel

DAY BEFORE

Method Rinse the cabbage or iceberg lettuce leaves and dry using paper towels. Heat the coconut oil in a frying pan and cook the chicken breast, whole. Once cooked, use two forks to pull the meat apart while it's warm. Sprinkle the chicken with the garlic and tamari and let cool.

Once the chicken cools, wet the rice paper sheets, one by one, in a large bowl of lukewarm water. Shake off the excess water and lay the sheets on a clean surface, such as a damp, clean tea towel on the counter or on a marble cutting board. Place one-sixth of the ingredients on one half of a rice paper sheet, starting with the mint, then a cabbage or lettuce leaf, chicken, a few cilantro leaves, bell pepper, carrot, cucumber, and some sesame seeds. Fold the roll in half and fold both sides inward, toward the middle. Roll the sheet up fully—tightly but carefully. Repeat with the remaining 5 sheets and ingredients. Place the spring rolls in a to-go container. And don't forget the dip!

power food on the go

Sushi on the Go

Making sushi is less work than you think. If you're going to take the time to make it, make enough for a couple of days. This veggie sushi is also great for sharing at a picnic or a party.

PREPARATION TIME
1½ hours

INGREDIENTS
(makes 4 sushi rolls)
* About 1¼ cups (8½ ounces, or 240 g) short-grain brown rice
* 2 tablespoons (30 ml) tamari
* ½ bell pepper, any color
* 1 avocado, peeled and pitted
* Small handful fresh basil leaves
* 7 ounces (200 g) carrot
* 4 nori sheets
* 4 small handfuls alfalfa sprouts
* 4 teaspoons sesame seeds
* Salt, to taste
* Sushi Dip (page 131)

KEEPS FOR
a maximum of 2 days in the fridge

SUPPLIES
bamboo rolling mat (optional)

Method Rinse the rice well in a sieve and let it drain for 10 minutes. Bring 10 fluid ounces (300 ml) water to a rolling boil and add the rice. Cook the rice according to the package instructions. Check to see if the rice is done and all the moisture has been absorbed. Add a splash of hot water if the rice is still not cooked and the pan is getting dry. Once cooked, stir the tamari into the rice and let cool fully. Speed this process up by giving the rice a careful stir every now and then.

Rinse the vegetables. Slice the bell pepper and the avocado into thin strips. Chop the basil into ribbons and grate the carrot. Spoon one-fourth of the rice on 1 nori sheet, spreading it evenly across the sheet, but leaving 1½ to 2 inches (4 to 5 cm) free of rice on one end. Lay strips of bell pepper, avocado, and grated carrot along the entire width of the nori sheet. Place some basil, alfalfa, sesame seeds, and a bit of salt on top of the vegetables. Roll the nori sheet tightly by hand or using your bamboo rolling mat. Wet the rice-free edge of the nori sheet and press it down to seal it.

Using a very sharp knife, slice the roll into pieces. Transfer to a storage container. Repeat with the remaining nori sheets and ingredients. Serve the sushi rolls with the dip.

Sushi Dip
recipe pg. 131

Letting the rice sit
for a bit makes it
stickier. Sushi rice
should actually be cooled
as quickly as possible.
In Japan, they often use fans...

A Sunday
well spent
brings a week
of content

Buckwheat Noodle Salad

*Soba noodles are made from **buckwheat**, a seed **full** of **amino acids**, and therefore a complete **protein** source. Plus, your body can easily **digest** it. The fish and **soy sauce** in this **recipe** give it a nice Asian **touch**.*

PRE-PREPARATION TIME
about 30 minutes

PREPARATION TIME
10 minutes

TOTAL TIME
40 minutes

INGREDIENTS
(serves 3)

* 9 ounces (250 g) green beans
* 5⅓ ounces (150 g) soba noodles (buckwheat)
* 9 ounces (250 g) cod fillet
* Juice of ½ lime
* Salt and freshly ground black pepper, to taste
* ½ teaspoon ground turmeric
* Coconut oil or ghee, for frying
* 1 small onion, finely chopped
* 1 clove garlic, finely chopped
* 4 scallions, finely chopped
* 2 inches (5 cm) fresh ginger, finely chopped
* 10½ ounces (300 g) shiitake mushrooms, thinly sliced
* 6 tablespoons plus 2 teaspoons (100 ml) coconut milk
* 1 teaspoon Veggie Powder Mix (page 137)
* 2 tablespoons (30 ml) tamari
* Pinch cayenne pepper
* Small handful bean sprouts

KEEPS FOR
2 days in the fridge

SUPPLIES
grill pan; food processor

Method Clean the green beans and cook them in boiling water until al dente. Drain. Cook the soba noodles in a pot of boiling water as well. Drain and transfer the cooked noodles to a sieve and rinse with cold water.

Heat the grill pan. Rub the cod with lime juice, salt, pepper, and turmeric. Grill the fish for 10 minutes, turning it carefully after 5 minutes. Heat 1 teaspoon coconut oil in a frying pan and sauté the onion, garlic, scallions, ginger, and mushrooms for 1 to 2 minutes. Stir in the coconut milk, veggie powder mix, tamari, cayenne, and green beans. Simmer for a few minutes, stirring occasionally.

Add the drained noodles, toss to combine, and transfer to a bowl. Place the fish on top of the noodles and vegetables and sprinkle with bean sprouts.

Macadamia Pesto
recipe pg. 135

Macadamia Pasta

The flavor combination produced by the nuts, basil, and acidic lime juice is amazing. This lunchtime pasta might just be my very favorite! And, after eating it, I'm always nicely satisfied and ready to take on the afternoon.

PREPARATION TIME
25 minutes

INGREDIENTS
(serves 2)
* 3½ ounces (100 g) peas, freshly shelled or frozen
* 5⅓ ounces (150 g) snap peas
* About 4½ ounces (125 g) black rice noodles
* 1 tablespoon (15 ml) fresh lime juice
* 1 tablespoon (15 g) tahini
* 2 teaspoons apple cider vinegar
* 1 teaspoon extra-virgin olive oil
* 1 avocado, peeled and pitted
* 1 tablespoon (7 g) hemp seeds
* About 1 cup (2⅔ ounces, or 75 g) mixed salad greens
* Salt, to taste
* 3 tablespoons (about 120 g) Macadamia Pesto (page 135)

KEEPS FOR
2 days in the fridge in an airtight container

Method Bring a large pot of water to a boil and cook the peas and snap peas for about 3 minutes until al dente. Drain in a colander, rinse with cold water, and let drain fully.

Bring another pot of water to a boil and cook the rice noodles until done, about 6 minutes (or according to package instructions), until soft, but not falling apart. Have a bowl of ice-cold water ready on the counter so you can transfer the noodles into the bowl after draining to stop the cooking process. Drain in a colander once again.

Make the tahini dressing by combining the lime juice, tahini, apple cider vinegar, and olive oil in a small jar with a tight-fitting lid. Chop the avocado into cubes. Place the drained rice noodles in a salad bowl and top with the peas, snap peas, and avocado.

Sprinkle with hemp seeds and take the salad to go with the dressing and macadamia pesto on the side.

Tip: Can't find black rice noodles? Just use another whole-grain variety!

snacks

Sometimes I'll spend an entire Sunday prepping snacks. Cookies, bars, chips . . . I like to make big batches at a time so I can store them or freeze them. Spend just one Sunday cooking your heart out and you'll profit from it for the week to come. You'll be able to grab something tasty and bring it with you on the go, every single day. You'll also steal the show with these snacks— should you choose to share them.

Granola Bars *(the chocolate version)*

*Here I go again with my **handy** snack bars—this **time** chocolate flavored! **Why** am I such a fan? It's incredibly **easy** to make **ten** at a time so you can **take** one in your **lunch** each **day** in the weeks to come. Easy **does** it.*

PREPARATION TIME
15 minutes
COOLING TIME
1 hour
TOTAL TIME
1 hour and 15 minutes

INGREDIENTS
(makes about 10 bars)
* 4¼ ounces (120 g) walnuts
* 5⅓ ounces (150 g) mixed nuts
* Slightly more than 8 ounces (230 g) Medjool dates, pitted
* 3½ ounces (100 g) whole oats
* 1½ ounces (40 g) barberry berries or other dried berries of choice—but note that the bars will be less sour
* 3 heaping tablespoons (16+ g) raw cacao powder
* 2 tablespoons (28 g) coconut oil, softened
* 1 tablespoon (20 g) maple syrup
* 1 teaspoon ground cinnamon
* ½ teaspoon salt

KEEPS FOR
1½ weeks in the fridge; you can also freeze them
SUPPLIES
food processor; large mixing bowl; parchment paper

SUNDAY PREP

Method Finely grind the walnuts in the food processor, being careful not to blend them into nut butter, and transfer to a large mixing bowl. Roughly chop the mixed nuts using a knife. Purée the dates in the food processor. Combine all the ingredients in the mixing bowl, mix well, and use your hands to knead the mixture into a large ball. Place the ball on a sheet of parchment paper and flatten using the outside of a spoon. Be sure to press down firmly, otherwise the bars will crumble. Slice into bars and refrigerate for at least 1 hour to firm them up.

Coconut Whipped
Cream recipe pg. 136

Delicious with a dollop
of coconut whipped cream!

Pecan Pie

This is the perfect pecan pie! This pie is secretly super easy to make and is a crowd pleaser at dinner parties with friends. Leftovers? Slice the pie into individual servings and freeze them. That way you can grab a sweet snack every now and then when you're in a hurry.

PREPARATION TIME
20 minutes

BAKING TIME
25 to 30 minutes

TOTALE TIJD
about 45 minutes

INGREDIENTS
(makes 1 pie)
For Crust:
* ¼ cup plus 1 teaspoon (about 2 ounces, or 60 g) coconut oil
* 7 ounces (200 g) Medjool dates, pitted
* 1 egg
* 14 ounces (400 g) almond flour or other flour of choice

For Filling:
* 14 ounces (400 g) pecans, halved
* 3 eggs
* 5 tablespoons (100 g) maple syrup
* ½ teaspoon unsweetened vanilla powder
* Pinch ground cardamom
* Salt, to taste
* Coconut Whipped Cream (page 136; optional)

KEEPS FOR
1 week in the fridge; can also be frozen

SUPPLIES
food processor; springform pan (9½ inches, or 24 cm diameter)

Method Preheat the oven to 350°F (180°C). Grease the springform pan with a bit of coconut oil.

To make the crust: Melt the remaining coconut oil in a pan, if necessary (do not let it get too warm). Add the dates to the food processor as well as egg, almond flour, and coconut oil. Blend until a large ball of dough forms. Transfer the dough to the prepared springform pan and press it down firmly to cover the bottom of the pan to form a crust.

Next, make the filling: Finely grind 7 ounces (200 g) of the pecans in the food processor. Beat the eggs in a large mixing bowl until light and fluffy. Add the ground nuts, remaining pecan halves, maple syrup, vanilla powder, cardamom, and salt to the eggs. Mix well and pour on top of the crust. You can also chop a few extra dates and sprinkle the pieces on top of the pie.

Bake the pie in the preheated oven for 25 to 30 minutes. Let cool. Slice into small pieces and store in the fridge. You can also freeze some of this pie, being sure to slice it into individual servings and store the pieces in airtight containers. That way you can take out a couple of slices at a time to thaw.Taking the pie with you? Leave it in the springform pan to help it keep its shape and cover it with a clean tea towel. Place the pie in a bag with a wide bottom, being sure to keep it upright!

Serve with coconut whipped cream (if using).

Tip: You can also use another type of flour for the crust. It's entirely up to you.

Food
on the go
makes you
glow

Chia Cookies

I'll admit it. I've taken a container of these cookies with me to work and eaten them all before lunchtime. Oops. It's a shame, since they keep for a month! It's a good plan to make a big batch of these at once so you're set for a while. But beware: They are so tasty!

PREPARATION TIME
about 20 minutes

BAKING TIME
10 minutes

TOTAL TIME
30 minutes

SUNDAY PREP

INGREDIENTS
(makes about 10 cookies)
* 1 tablespoon chia seeds
* 2¾ ounces (80 g) oat flour or other flour of choice
* 3½ ounces (100 g) coconut sugar
* 1 teaspoon baking soda
* 1 tablespoon (15 ml) fresh lemon juice
* 9 ounces (250 g) almond butter or mixed-nut butter with added salt

KEEPS FOR
about 1 month in an airtight container

SUPPLIES
baking sheet lined with parchment paper

Method Soak the chia seeds for 15 minutes in 3 tablespoons (45 ml) water. Meanwhile, combine the flour, sugar, and baking soda in a mixing bowl.

Preheat the oven to 400°F (200°C). Once the chia seeds absorb all the water, combine them with the lemon juice and almond butter in a separate bowl. Stir well and add the wet ingredients to the dry ingredients. Knead the mixture using your hands until a ball forms. Pinch off bits of dough and form them into small patties in the palm of your hand, repeating until the dough is gone. Lay the patties on the prepared baking sheet, place the sheet in the preheated oven, and bake for 10 minutes. Cool the cookies and enjoy!

Golden Milk
recipe pg. 127

Gingerbread Snack *photo pg. 117*

I love cashews. Add some maple syrup and gingerbread spices and you've got a holiday snack that you can indulge in guilt free.

PREPARATION TIME
5 minutes
BAKING TIME
10 to 15 minutes
TOTAL TIME
20 minutes

INGREDIENTS
(makes 1 small container [about 3½ ounces, or 100 g])
* 3½ ounces (100 g) raw cashews
* 2 heaping tablespoons gingerbread spice mix
* 1 tablespoon (20 g) maple syrup
* Pinch salt

KEEPS FOR
1 month in a dry, airtight container
SUPPLIES
baking sheet lined with parchment paper

SUNDAY PREP

Method Preheat the oven to 400°F (200°C). Combine the cashews, gingerbread spices, maple syrup, and salt in a bowl and toss thoroughly. Spread the nuts on the prepared baking sheet and place it in the middle of the preheated oven for 10 to 15 minutes. Give the nuts a stir after about 5 minutes. Keep an eye on the nuts to make sure they don't burn. Let cool fully and store them in a jar with a tight-fitting lid. Tasty on the go or on the couch.

Date-Gingerbread Balls *photo pg. 117*

Sweet and spice and *everything* nice. These *balls* are actually best eaten when it's *cold* outside. The gingerbread spices *warm* you and the dates give you *energy*.

PREPARATION TIME
about 40 minutes

INGREDIENTS
(makes about 16 balls)
* 9 ounces (250 g) Medjool dates, pitted
* 3½ ounces (about 1 cup, or 100 g) almond flour
* 1 tablespoon (14 g) coconut oil, softened or melted
* 2 teaspoons gingerbread spice mix
* Pinch salt
* ½ cup (1½ ounces, or 40 g) instant oatmeal
* 1 tablespoon raw cacao powder (optional)

KEEPS FOR
5 days in the fridge, if you can resist them! Or freeze them.

SUPPLIES
food processor

Method Place the dates in the food processor and purée them. Add the remaining ingredients, *except* the oatmeal and cacao powder, and blend again. Remove the blade from the bowl of the food processor, add the oatmeal, and use your hands to form small balls of dough. I usually roll them in a bit of cacao powder. Super tasty, but skipping this step also produces a totally yummy result!

Salty Snack

Sometimes your body just screams for something salty and, when it does, these little balls are just what you need. The addition of puréed sweet potato and walnuts makes these savory snacks nutritious, too. If you store them in the fridge, you can grab a couple every so often.

PREPARATION TIME
10 minutes
BAKING TIME
20 minutes
TOTAL TIME
30 minutes

INGREDIENTS
(makes about 12 balls)
* 14 ounces (400 g) Sweet Potato Purée (page 135)
* 1 small onion, finely chopped
* Coconut oil or ghee, for frying
* 3 tablespoons (21 g) coconut flour or other flour of choice
* 1 tablespoon dried oregano
* 2 teaspoons ground cumin
* 1 teaspoon Red Curry Paste (page 136)
* Pinch salt
* ½ teaspoon freshly ground black pepper
* Small handful walnuts, finely chopped

KEEPS FOR
4 days in the fridge
SUPPLIES
food processor; baking sheet lined with parchment paper

SUNDAY PREP

Method Preheat the oven to 350°F (180°C). Place the sweet potato purée in a bowl. Sauté the onion in a bit of coconut oil in a frying pan until glassy. Combine the onion, coconut flour, oregano, cumin, and red curry paste with the sweet potato purée. Season to taste with salt and add the pepper and chopped walnuts to the mixture. Using your hands, form small balls out of the dough. Place them on the prepared baking sheet, put the sheet in the preheated oven, and bake for about 20 minutes.

salty
Snack

Sweet Potato Chips

It's easy to buy a bag of chips when you're en route . . . but it's so much healthier and tastier just to make them yourself. I don't think I need to remind you I'm in love with sweet potatoes. These paper-thin snacks are just the ticket when you're craving something savory.

PREPARATION TIME
5 minutes
BAKING TIME
20 to 30 minutes
TOTAL TIME
25 to 35 minutes

INGREDIENTS
(makes 1 container [about 32 ounces, or 907 g])
* 3 sweet potatoes
* 1 tablespoon (14 g) coconut oil
* 2 teaspoons thyme, dried or fresh
* Pinch salt

KEEPS FOR
1 week in an airtight container
SUPPLIES
mandoline or cheese slicer; baking sheet

SUNDAY PREP

Method Preheat the oven to 320°F (160°C). Scrub the sweet potatoes under the tap and dry thoroughly. Slice them into paper-thin slices using a mandoline or cheese slicer and place them in a bowl. Melt the coconut oil, if necessary, and add it to the sweet potato slices along with the thyme and a bit of salt. Toss carefully to combine.

Spread the raw chips on a baking sheet. Make sure they are not layered on top of each other; otherwise they won't get crispy. Bake until crispy, 20 to 30 minutes (depending on your oven). Keep your eye on their progress to make sure they don't burn. Flip the chips about 10 minutes in.

drinks

Most drinks are best consumed fresh. Sometimes I secretly get on my bike and ride to a juice bar, but it really doesn't take long to make your own smoothie or juice. If you like to make your own juices, but don't always have the time (or motivation) to drag out the blender in the morning, make a big bottle ahead of time, store it in the fridge, and pour some into a smaller bottle each morning to take with you.

Mint-Chocolate Drink

The combination of mint and cacao is so tasty! Drink it in the morning to start your day off fresh and sharp. The banana makes this drink quite filling.

PREPARATION TIME
5 minutes

INGREDIENTS
(makes 2 smoothies [20¼ fluid ounces, or 600 ml])
* 1 lime
* 1 banana, peeled
* 13½ fluid ounces (400 ml) coconut milk
* 6 tablespoons plus 2 teaspoons (100 ml) water
* 2 tablespoons fresh mint leaves
* Small handful fresh spinach
* 2 teaspoons peppermint extract
* 2 teaspoons raw cacao powder

KEEPS FOR
1 day
SUPPLIES
blender; jar with tight-fitting lid

Method Squeeze the lime juice into the blender. Add all the remaining ingredients and mix until creamy. Pour in a to-go jar.

Date-Gingerbread Balls
recipe pg. 109

Gingerbread Snack
recipe pg. 108

Happy Spinach Smoothie photo pg. 122

A creamy smoothie with cacao that prompts your body to release happiness chemicals. The addition of spinach ensures you get an extra vitamin boost, which makes your body happy, too.

PREPARATION TIME
5 minutes

INGREDIENTS
(makes 2 smoothies [20¼ fluid ounces, or 600 ml])
* 10 fluid ounces (300 ml) oat milk or other plant-based milk of choice
* 2 bananas, peeled
* 1 avocado, peeled and pitted
* Large handful fresh baby spinach
* 1 tablespoon raw cacao powder
* Pinch unsweetened vanilla powder

KEEPS FOR
2 days in the fridge
SUPPLIES
blender

Method Combine all the ingredients in the blender and mix until a super-creamy tasty smoothie forms. Pour your happiness into 2 to-go cups and take one with you. Put the other cup of instant happiness in the fridge for tomorrow.

Iced Mint Tea *photo pg. 122*

I often bring sprigs of fresh mint with me when I go out. I'll find a glass of hot water one way or another and then I instantly have a tasty tea. It's even tastier to drink your mint tea cold though. Add a big spoonful of honey and some fennel seeds and you've made yourself a heavenly iced tea.

PREPARATION TIME
10 minutes

INGREDIENTS
(makes about 1 quart [1 liter])
* About 3 heaping tablespoons (20 g) fresh mint leaves
* 1 tablespoon fennel seeds
* Juice of ½ lemon
* Raw honey, to taste

KEEPS FOR
1 day in the fridge

SUPPLIES
blender; large bottle

DAY BEFORE

Method Bring 4 cups (1 liter) water to a boil and combine it with the fresh mint in a teapot. Let stand for 10 minutes. Strain the mint leaves out of the tea, pour the tea into the blender, add the lemon juice and honey, and blend. Pour the finished product into a large bottle and let cool fully.

My
limit is
beyond
the
sky

Iced Mint Tea
recipe pg. 119

Happy Spinach
Smoothie
recipe pg. 118

Strawberry Smoothie (with avocado and oatmeal)

Sweet, healthy, filling, and pink. I'm in love with this smoothie!
Preferably made with fresh strawberries but, if they're not in season,
frozen is delicious, too.

PREPARATION TIME
7 minutes

INGREDIENTS
(makes 2 smoothies [20¼ fluid
ounces, or 600 ml])
* 9 ounces (250 g) fresh
strawberries, hulled
(use frozen in winter)
* 1 avocado, peeled and pitted
* ½ lemon
* ½ banana
* ½ teaspoon ground cinnamon
* 1 tablespoon (5 g)
instant oatmeal
* 1 teaspoon (raw) honey

KEEPS FOR
1 day
SUPPLIES
blender; bottles

Method Add all the ingredients to the blender and mix until creamy. Pour into 1 or 2 bottles and take them to go.

power food on the go

Cashew Milk

You can substitute homemade nut milk in any recipe that calls for regular dairy. Think desserts, smoothies, or with your granola. It's also much creamier!

SOAKING TIME
about 4 hours

PREPARATION TIME
5 minutes

TOTAL TIME
Just over 4 hours

DAY BEFORE

INGREDIENTS
(makes about 1 quart [1 liter])
* 5⅓ ounces (150 g) raw cashews
* 1½ teaspoons unsweetened vanilla powder
* Pinch salt

KEEPS FOR
3 to 4 days in the fridge

SUPPLIES
blender; milk bottles

Method Soak the cashews in twice as much water as the cashews for at least 4 hours. Rinse and drain. Combine the nuts with 3¾ cups plus 1 tablespoon (30½ fluid ounces, or 900 ml) fresh water, the vanilla powder, and salt in the blender. Process for about 2 minutes. Pour the cashew milk into the bottles.

Tip: Don't like the pulp? Strain the milk using a sieve before you transfer it to the bottles. The pulp that remains can be used for a smoothie.

You can also warm the milk if you have the opportunity.

Granola recipe pg. 31

Drink Your Veggies *photo pg. 88*

*Hyper healthy! A **shot** of greens that gives your **immune system** a boost and tunes up your **motor**. **Ginger** and apple make this **juice** nice and fresh. You can keep this in the fridge for up to **three** days, so grab a **bottle** and go.*

PREPARATION TIME
10 minutes

INGREDIENTS
(makes 2 to 3 juices [about 1 quart, or 1 liter])
* 3½ ounces (100 g) fresh spinach
* 4 celery stalks
* 2 apples
* 1 cucumber
* 1 organic lemon
* About ¾ ounce (20 g) fresh ginger

KEEPS FOR
3 days in the fridge
SUPPLIES
juicer; 2 or 3 bottles with tight-fitting lids

LAST MINUTE

Method Rinse all the ingredients and chop them into small pieces. Process them in a juicer to make a super-healthy juice. If you remove the seeds from the apple and lemon before juicing you can use the pulp in a smoothie or add it to pancakes. Pour the juice into bottles, seal with the lids, and place in the fridge. Health and happiness guaranteed!

Golden Milk *photo pg. 107*

When I was learning about Ayurveda, I discovered this drink with cardamom, ginger, turmeric, and honey—and fell instantly in love. While drinking it warm makes you feel very relaxed, drinking it cold also creates a Zen moment in your day.

PREPARATION TIME
5 minutes

INGREDIENTS
(makes 2 bottles [20¼ fluid ounces, or 600 ml])
* 2 cups (500 ml) almond milk
* 2½ teaspoons ground turmeric
* 2 teaspoons raw honey
* 1 (1-inch, or 2.5 cm) piece fresh ginger
* ½ teaspoon ground cinnamon
* ½ teaspoon ground cardamom

KEEPS FOR
3 days in the fridge

SUPPLIES
blender; 2 bottles with tight-fitting lids

Method Add all the ingredients to the blender and mix until smooth and fully combined. Pour into the bottles, seal, refrigerate, and drink whenever you feel like it. The milk contains little bits of ginger. If you don't like this, substitute 1 teaspoon ground ginger for the fresh ginger.

Just let me ride and no one gets hurt

Almond Dressing

INGREDIENTS

* ½ cup (120 ml) sesame oil
* 5 tablespoons (70 g) almond butter
* ¼ cup (60 ml) fresh lime juice
* ¼ cup (60 ml) tamari
* ¼ cup (60 ml) water
* 4 teaspoons (26.6 g) maple syrup
* 2 teaspoons freshly ground black pepper
* ½ teaspoon salt

SUPPLIES
jam jar

Method Combine all the ingredients in a jam jar. Close the lid, shake, and it's done!

Chocolate Sauce

INGREDIENTS

* 7 ounces (200 g) Medjool dates, pitted
* 5 tablespoons (75 ml) water
* 2 tablespoons raw cacao powder
* Pinch unsweetened vanilla powder
* Pinch salt

SUPPLIES
food processor; Weck jar

Method Combine all the ingredients in a food processor and blend until a smooth sauce forms. Keep refrigerated in a Weck jar.

ALL OF THESE DIPS
keep for 3 to 5 days in the fridge.

Almond Sauce

INGREDIENTS

* 5⅓ ounces (150 g) almond butter
* 3 tablespoons (45 ml) tamari
* ¼ cup (120 ml) water

Method Combine all the ingredients in a bowl and stir well with a fork.

....

Nut Dressing

INGREDIENTS

* 2 tablespoons (28 g) mixed nut butter
* 1 tablespoon (15 ml) extra-virgin olive oil
* 1 tablespoon (15 ml) fresh lemon juice
* 1 teaspoon maple syrup
* Salt and freshly ground black pepper, to taste

Method Stir the nut butter, olive oil, lemon juice, and maple syrup into a dressing. Season to taste with salt and pepper.

....

The Best Dip Ever

INGREDIENTS

* 6 tablespoons plus 2 teaspoons (100 ml) water
* 2 tablespoons (28 g) organic peanut butter
* 1 tablespoon (15 ml) tamari
* 1 teaspoon sambal
* 1 teaspoon maple syrup
* 1 teaspoon apple cider vinegar
* ⅛ ounce fresh ginger, finely chopped

Method Combine everything in a to-go container. Use a fork to stir it together.

Cashew Dressing

INGREDIENTS

* 6⅓ ounces (180 g) raw cashews
* 6 tablespoons plus 2 teaspoons (100 ml) extra-virgin olive oil
* 3 tablespoons (45 ml) fresh lemon juice
* 2 cloves garlic
* Salt, to taste

SUPPLIES

food processor; jar with tight-fitting lid

Method Add all the ingredients to the food processor and blend for 2 minutes until a deliciously creamy dressing forms. Refrigerate in a jar with a tight-fitting lid.

....

Sushi Dip

INGREDIENTS

* 2 tablespoons (28 g) Homemade Mayonnaise (page 134)
* 2 teaspoons wasabi
* 1 tablespoon (15 ml) fresh lime juice

Method Stir the ingredients together to combine.

....

Tahini Syrup

INGREDIENTS

* ½ cup plus 2 tablespoons (150 g) tahini
* ½ cup plus 2 tablespoons (53 g) raw cacao powder
* 4 teaspoons (26.6 g) maple syrup

Method Stir the ingredients together to combine.

Red Curry Paste

I always have a jar of this paste in the fridge or freezer. It adds heat to any dish.

Macadamia Pesto

I like to change things up by experimenting with different nuts and herbs in my pesto. Everybody loves it! Whip up a jar in no time.

Sweet Potato Purée

You can use this purée in so many recipes. Serve it as a side dish, add it to a casserole or granola, and use it to give your snack balls a bit more body.

Coconut Whipped Cream

A surprising variation on regular whipped cream and just as easy to make. It's best on homemade muffins, cakes, or pies.

Fish Herb Mix

Store-bought herb mixes tend to be expensive and sometimes contain ingredients that you'd rather not eat. I like to make it myself.

Veggie Powder Mix

I use this mix instead of bouillon cubes. Handy (and tastier), and you know exactly what's in it.

Homemade mayonnaise

There's nothing better than homemade mayo! Make a big jar of it. It keeps well in the fridge.

Basics

Homemade Mayonnaise

PREPARATION TIME
about 20 minutes

INGREDIENTS
(makes 1 jar [about 8 ounces, or 227 g])
* 3 cloves garlic
* 2 egg yolks
* 1 tablespoon (15 ml) fresh lemon juice
* 1 teaspoon ground ginger
* 1 teaspoon mustard
* Sea salt and freshly ground black pepper, to taste
* Pinch dried parsley
* 6¾ fluid ounces (200 ml) rice oil

KEEPS FOR
1 week in the fridge

SUPPLIES
mortar and pestle; immersion blender

Method Grind the garlic fine using the mortar and pestle and transfer it to a tall liquid measuring cup. Add the remaining ingredients, *except* the rice oil. Place the immersion blender in the measuring cup and begin blending while slowly adding the oil, drop by drop. Once the mixture begins to thicken, add the remaining oil a bit more quickly until all of it is integrated. Season to taste with salt and pepper. Use the mayo right away or refrigerate until you're ready to use it.

Make sure that the pesto is level in the jar. Then top the pesto with two tablespoons of olive oil to seal it off and keep it fresher for longer.

Macadamia Pesto

PREPARATION TIME
15 minutes

INGREDIENTS
(makes about 9 ounces [250 g])
* 4 tablespoons (60 ml) extra-virgin olive oil, divided
* 4¼ ounces (120 g) roasted macadamia nuts
* 3½ ounces (100 g) hard goat cheese, grated
* About 1¼ cups (1¾ ounces, or 50 g) fresh basil leaves
* ¼ cup (60 ml) oat milk
* 1 tablespoon (15 ml) fresh lemon juice
* 1 clove garlic
* ½ teaspoon freshly ground black pepper
* Salt, to taste

KEEPS FOR
1 week in the fridge in an airtight container
SUPPLIES
food processor; Weck jar

Method Combine 2 tablespoons olive oil with the remaining ingredients in the food processor and pulse until coarsely blended. Transfer to a Weck jar and add the last 2 tablespoons olive oil on top before storing.

SUNDAY PREP

Sweet Potato Purée

PREPARATION TIME
3 minutes
BAKING TIME
45 minutes
TOTAL TIME
about 50 minutes

INGREDIENTS
(makes about 10½ ounces [300 g])
* 17½ ounces (500 g) sweet potatoes
* Coconut oil, for greasing

KEEPS FOR
a maximum of 5 days in the fridge; can also be frozen
SUPPLIES
roasting pan; food processor or blender; airtight container

Method Preheat the oven to 350°F (180°C). Slice the sweet potatoes into large pieces and toss them in a bit of coconut oil. Divide the sweet potatoes evenly across the roasting pan, place the pan in the preheated oven, and roast for about 45 minutes. Check for doneness using a fork. Once cooked, let the sweet potatoes cool, remove the skins, and blend in the food processor (or blender) until creamy. You can also mash them. Keep the purée in an airtight container.

Coconut Whipped Cream

PRE-PREPARATION TIME
a minimum of 12 hours
PREPARATION TIME
5 minutes
TOTAL TIME
more than 12 hours

INGREDIENTS
(makes 1 jar [about 16 ounces or 454 g])
* 1 can (13.5 fluid ounces, or 400 ml) full-fat coconut milk
* 1 tablespoon (20 g) maple syrup
* Pinch unsweetened vanilla powder

KEEPS FOR
3 days in the fridge
SUPPLIES
hand mixer or stand mixer

Method Place the can of coconut milk in the fridge overnight (a minimum of 12 hours). The water and the cream need to separate. Open the can the next day and remove the coconut cream (the top layer) using a spoon, transferring the cream to a bowl. Add the maple syrup and the vanilla to the cream and beat using a mixer until smooth and creamy. Use a piping bag to ice your muffins, cakes, pies, or other desserts, if you'd like.

Red Curry Paste

PREPARATION TIME
15 minutes

INGREDIENTS
(makes 1 jar [16 ounces, or 454 g])
* 1 lemon
* 2 medium-size red onions
* 3 cloves garlic
* 1 red chilli pepper
* 1 (1¼-inch, or 3 cm) piece fresh ginger
* 6 tablespoons (90 ml) peanut oil or rice oil
* 3½ ounces (100 g) tomato paste
* 2 tablespoons garam masala
* 2 tablespoons ground turmeric
* 1 tablespoon paprika
* 1 tablespoon mustard seeds, ground
* 2 teaspoons curry powder
* 2 teaspoons freshly ground black pepper
* 1 teaspoon Laos powder
* 1 teaspoon ground coriander

KEEPS FOR
at least 1 week in the fridge
SUPPLIES
food processor or immersion blender; jar with tight-fitting lid

Method Zest the lemon, finely chop the onions, garlic, red chilli pepper, and ginger. Combine with the remaining ingredients. Transfer to the food processor (or use an immersion blender) and blend the ingredients until a smooth paste forms. And that's it! Spoon the curry into a jar with a tight-fitting lid to store.

Use this mix to add flavor to soups and other dishes. Use 1 teaspoon for every 6¾ fluid ounces (2 dl) of water or sauce. To make a bouillon to drink, combine 1 teaspoon with 6¾ to 8½ fluid ounces (2 to 2.5 dl) boiling water.

Fish Herb Mix

PREPARATION TIME
5 minutes

INGREDIENTS
(makes 1 jar [about 7 tablespoons, or about 20 g])
* 2 tablespoons dried thyme
* 1 tablespoon dried basil
* 1 tablespoon dried parsley
* 1 tablespoon ground rosemary
* 2 teaspoons freshly ground black pepper
* 2 teaspoons dried marjoram
* 1 teaspoon dried oregano
* 1 teaspoon celery salt
* 1 teaspoon garlic powder

KEEPS FOR
more than 1 year

Method Add all the ingredients to a jar, put the lid on, and shake or stir with a spoon to combine.

Veggie Powder Mix

PREPARATION TIME
5 minutes

INGREDIENTS
(makes 1 jar [about 5 tablespoons, or about 39 g])
* 1 tablespoon onion powder
* 2 teaspoons freeze-dried garlic or garlic powder
* 2 teaspoons dried thyme
* 2 teaspoons ground turmeric
* 2 teaspoons salt, ground
* 1 teaspoon ground rosemary
* 1 teaspoon ground cumin
* 1 teaspoon freshly ground black pepper
* ½ teaspoon ground nutmeg

KEEPS FOR
more than 1 year

Method Add all the ingredients to a jar, put the lid on, and shake or stir with a spoon to combine.

Index

Dreams do come true

Another dream has come true ... I was so inspired to make something great for all the enthusiastic #powerfoodies out there who shared their Power Food creations and kept asking me for new recipes. You guys believe in me and that gives me such an amazing amount of energy. A third book was definitely in order and I hope it's the answer to, at least, some of your questions. I love you guys!

Before I give myself all the credit, I did not create this book on my own. I worked on this little gem with the very same power team behind *Power Food* and *Power Food from Friesland to New York*. Thank you, sweet Bülent, Anne, Tanja, Renske, Cecile, Pim, Lieke, Yvonne, and Unieboek|Het Spectrum. When we started on this project, we thought we'd be working on a short, little book. But thanks to your effort and skills, the book took on a life of its own. I'm so proud of us! I am endlessly grateful. I couldn't do it without you. Just so you know. Thank you to the Quarto Group for publishing this book in English. A big dream come true!

And finally, someone I could never forget because he supports me unconditionally, through thick and thin, my true love, Sid. Thank you for the nudge. *Ik hâld fan dy!*

Love,
Rens